Trees Are Made of Gas

Trees Are Made of Gas

The Story of Carbon and Climate

by **Kirk Johnson**
and **Mary Ann Bonnell**

CHICAGO
REVIEW
PRESS

Text © 2007 Kirk Johnson and Mary Ann Bonnell
Illustrations © 2007 Mary Ann Bonnell

All rights reserved
First Chicago Review Press edition published 2021

Published by Chicago Review Press Incorporated
814 North Franklin Street
Chicago, Illinois 60610
ISBN 978-1-68275-274-6

Design: Ann W. Douden
Editorial: Faith Marcovecchio, Haley Berry

Printed in the United States of America
5 4 3 2 1

Library of Congress Cataloging-in-Publication Data
for the previous edition is as follows:

Johnson, Kirk R.
 Gas trees and car turds : a kids' guide to the roots
of global warming / by Kirk Johnson and Mary
Ann Bonnell.
 p. cm.
 ISBN 978-1-55591-666-4 (pbk.)
 1. Atmospheric carbon dioxide–Juvenile literature.
2. Carbon cycle (Biogeochemistry)–Juvenile
literature. 3. Global warming–Juvenile literature.
I. Bonnell, Mary Ann. II. Title.
 QC879.8J64 2007
 577'.144–dc22
 2007017268

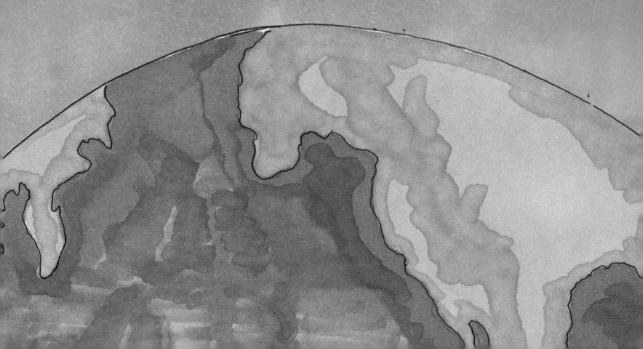

Meet See-oh-too

Carbon

Oxygen

Oxygen

Alias: carbon dioxide, CO_2
Molecular Weight: 44
Size: 76 million per inch
Source: volcanoes, **combustion**, or **respiration**

See-oh-too is someone you may not have seen or heard about before, but he is a busy, influential guy, someone you should get to know and understand. He is a simple **molecule** made up of one **carbon** atom (his head) and two **oxygen** atoms (his shoes). See-oh-too is an invisible **gas** in the air around you. There are only 380 See-oh-too molecules in every million molecules of air. See-oh-too gas can also dissolve in liquids—you can see it bubbling to the surface of a glass of pop. While he is mostly invisible to us, you may have spotted him in his **solid** form, **dry ice**.

Why is he so busy?

As you will soon see, See-oh-too gets
around, cycling his way through trees,
animals, water, and sky. To understand
the roots of **global warming**, you need
to get to know See-oh-too, how he
cycles, and how much control we have
over his adventures in our **atmosphere**.
For a little, invisible guy, See-oh-too
can cause big changes on our planet.
To get to the roots of this, let's begin
with a tree.

What are trees made of?

If you look at a tree, you will see lots of different parts. Trees have wooden roots, trunks, branches, and bark as well as leaves, flowers, fruits, seeds, and pollen.

This maple tree has hard wood, big-lobed leaves, and helicopter seeds. It makes a sweet sap that can be cooked down into maple syrup. Do you ever wonder where trees get the ingredients to make all this great stuff?

It is easy to think that a tree makes all this stuff
from ingredients it finds in the ground.

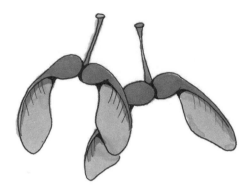

When you plant a maple seed,
that seed starts to grow.

Given water, **air**, and sun,
that seedling will become a tree.

Given the right ingredients, and about 80 years, the maple tree might grow to be 50 feet tall and weigh 4,000 pounds.

If you separated the 4,000 pounds of tree into **atoms**,
1,760 pounds would be carbon atoms,
1,760 pounds would be oxygen atoms,
240 pounds would be hydrogen atoms, and
240 pounds would be other minerals.

Did this 4,000 pounds of tree stuff come from the ground?

Trees are made of gas

To understand where a tree gets its ingredients, you need to understand how a tree produces food and grows. Humans eat food. Trees, on the other hand, make their own food. They do this by grabbing See-oh-too out of the air and taking his oxygen shoes off. Without his shoes, See-oh-too is just a carbon atom. His carbon and oxygen atoms are used to form the basic building blocks of trees. So, if you really think about it, trees are made of gas.

Soil Minerals

Oxygen

Carbon

How to make a tree

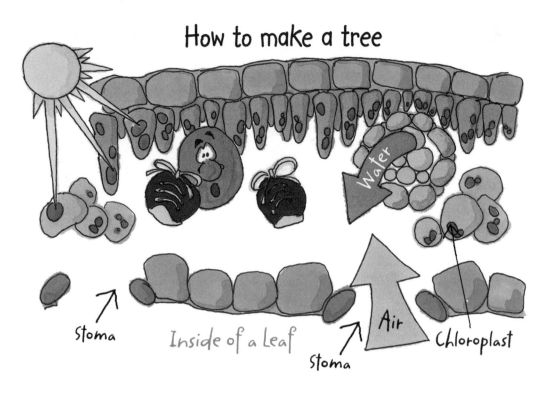

Stoma

Inside of a Leaf

Air

Stoma

Chloroplast

A tree removes See-oh-too's oxygen shoes in a process called **photosynthesis**, which uses energy from the sun and water. Trees pull water and a few minerals up out of the soil from their roots to their leaves through an internal plumbing system.

Leaves have holes, called **stomata**, that allow air—which contains See-oh-too—to come into the leaf. Inside the leaf, in **chloroplasts**, the tree grabs energy from the sun, breaks up the water it pulled from the ground, and uses the energy to pull See-oh-too's shoes off and make tree parts.

For these reasons, almost all of the weight of a tree (about 95 percent) comes from water from the roots and See-oh-too from the air that has been turned into tree parts using the energy of the sun. Even though trees grow in the soil, they don't use much of the soil to grow. They actually get most of their food from the air.

How to turn a tree back into gas

Will See-oh-too ever see his oxygen shoes again? The answer is yes, but how and when depends on what happens to the tree and its parts.

A dead tree in a forest can fall over and rot away.

Lightning or a person can start a forest fire that will burn up lots of trees.

A dead tree in a swamp can fall over and get buried in the mud.

But what does any of this have to do with See-oh-too's shoes?

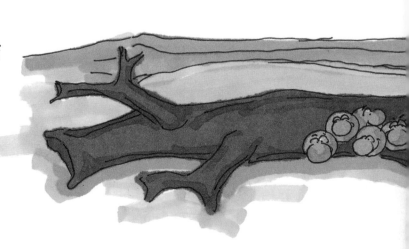

Rot it

Trees that die and fall over in the forest,
as well as trees that have been
chopped down and used
to make other things,
eventually rot away. Living
things such as funguses, insects,
and bacteria slowly chew away
at the stored energy in the trees,
and, in a process called respiration,
See-oh-too gets his oxygen shoes
back, floating away from the tree
and into thin air.

Burn it

Nature or humans may burn a tree or an
entire forest. In a process called combustion,
the burning carbon in a tree is reunited
with its oxygen shoes, releasing
See-oh-too, and many others just like
him, into the air all at
once, as well as a lot of
energy in the form of heat.

Bury it

Trees that grow in swamps are likely to get buried in the mud before they can rot or burn, leaving all those carbons trapped without their oxygen shoes, potentially for millions of years.

If that tree continues to get buried, over time those layers of mud and sand can get really thick. All that weight presses down on the buried trees and turns them into **coal**. Coal is a solid black rock made of squished dead, buried trees.

Coal is buried sunlight

Dead trees have been getting buried for over 350 million years. That's a lot of buried trees. Buried with those trees is a whole lot of energy, which originally came from the sun. The energy lies in the **bonds** made when the sun's energy was used to strip See-oh-too's oxygen shoes off. Those bonds only got stronger when the buried tree was squished and changed into coal.

Freeing the energy of ancient sunlight

Humans started digging up and burning coal hundreds of years ago. At first, energy from burning coal was used to heat homes, bend metals, or cook food. In the 1700s, people started burning coal to run machines in factories. Now we burn coal in power plants, where the released energy creates **electricity**, which is delivered to homes, offices, and stores.

The electricity that powers the lightbulbs in your house probably came from undoing the bonds in coal and giving See-oh-too his oxygen shoes back.

How much coal do we burn?

In the United States today, we burn a lot of coal, more than one billion tons a year. A ton of coal takes up about as much space as a refrigerator. Can you imagine a billion refrigerators? A billion refrigerators would fill the average football stadium more than 500 times.

Burning a billion tons of coal releases more than two billion tons of See-oh-too into the air every year.

What does nature do with all that See-oh-too?

While it seems like See-oh-too has not been very busy
or influential since he lost his oxygen shoes,
just wait until you see what he can do now
that he has them again.

What will See-oh-too do now that he is free?

The answer depends on where he floats off to and
how many other molecules of See-oh-too there are.

Warming up the globe

While See-oh-too may not seem very busy floating up there in the atmosphere, this is where he can be very influential. In addition to being colorless and odorless, See-oh-too is also a **greenhouse gas**. Like a blanket, See-oh-too traps heat that radiates from the Earth's surface into the Earth's atmosphere. The more See-oh-too there is in the atmosphere, the more insulating it can do.

If we look back in time, when See-oh-too was relatively rare in the sky, there was not as much of an insulating blanket and the cooler Earth experienced ice ages.

When See-oh-too levels in the atmosphere increased, the ice retreated, sea levels rose, and we had overall warmer times on Earth. The last ice age ended 11,500 years ago.

It is important to remember that when you give See-oh-too his oxygen shoes back, particularly when you give a whole lot of See-oh-toos their shoes back all at once, they can influence the temperature of the whole planet and cause global warming.

In a tree or in the sea

See-oh-too has been cycling in and out of the atmosphere for billions of years.

One way to remove See-oh-too from the air is to get him to make tree parts again.

If See-oh-too floats from the atmosphere toward a leaf, he may be sucked back into the leaf, stripped of his oxygen shoes, and turned into tree parts again.

In addition to making tree parts, some See-oh-too may leave the air and take a dip in the ocean. When See-oh-too dissolves in seawater, he can be captured and incorporated into the shells of marine animals or he can be combined with energy from the sun to grow marine plants.

Plankton is made of gas, too

The smallest of marine plants float
around in the water and are called **plankton**.
These tiny drifters look nothing like plants,
but they get their energy in the same
way as trees.

Plant plankton grow by using water and the sun's energy to take See-oh-too's oxygen shoes off. Once his oxygen shoes are removed, See-oh-too puts his carbon head together with other atoms and builds plant plankton parts.

How long will See-oh-too be stored in plankton? As with a tree, the answer to this question depends on what happens to these tiny plants.

Eat it

Plant plankton is at the bottom of the marine food
chain. When marine animals eat plant plankton,
the stored energy can build clams,
fish, sharks, and even
whales.

Rot it

Not all plankton is eaten. Dead plankton may rot as it sinks to the bottom of the ocean. In this way, a few See-oh-toos at a time get their oxygen shoes back and float away, free to roam the ocean or gas back out into the air.

Bury it

Sometimes plankton falls to the bottom of the ocean and gets buried. When plant plankton gets buried in the seafloor mud, See-oh-too may find himself waiting for his shoes for a long, long time.

Oil is buried sunlight, too

If the plankton are buried deeply enough, the layers of mud
surrounding the plankton will turn into rock. The weight
of the overlying rock squishes the buried plankton. Heat
and pressure cooks the buried plankton and turns it into
oil or **natural gas**. Usually the plankton has to be buried at
least two-and-a-half miles deep before the temperature and
pressure are high enough to make the kind of bonds
it takes to make oil or natural gas.

Oil on the move

Unlike coal, oil and natural gas can move around under the earth and find their way into sandy layers.

Sometimes oil even finds its way back to the surface. The La Brea Tar Pits in California is a place where oil seeped to the surface 38,000 years ago, trapping thousands of animals, including a whole lot of mammoths.

Oil makes things move

As with coal, there is a whole lot of energy stored in the bonds between the carbon atoms that make up oil. Humans first used this energy when they burned oil in lamps, reuniting lots of See-oh-toos with their oxygen shoes and setting them free into the air.

Humans use **refineries** to modify oil into **gasoline**. Humans invented **combustion engines**, which could use the energy trapped in gasoline to power cars, planes, lawn mowers, scooters, chain saws, and anything else with a motor.

Each time we travel in a car, mow the lawn, or cruise around on a motorized scooter, we free a great number of See-oh-toos from their ancient bonds and send them into the atmosphere.

How much oil do we use?

The United States uses about 7.3 billion barrels of oil a year.
This is a lot of oil. It's enough to fill a football stadium 636 times
or to fill nearly half a million Olympic-sized swimming pools.

Thinking in terms of turds

If you could collect all the See-oh-too gas released from burning
one gallon of gasoline, it would easily fill a backyard bouncy castle.
If that See-oh-too came out as visible chunks of carbon—we'll call
them turds—there would be about five pounds of car turds lying
on the ground for every gallon of gasoline used.

5 lbs. carbon
in 1 gal. gas
+
14 lbs. oxygen
added when gas burns
=
19 lbs. See-oh-too
(or 5 lbs. car turds)

car turds

Many people get annoyed with how many turds a Canada goose can make in a day, which is a little less than two pounds. If your family uses just one gallon of gasoline a day, you've already left behind more than twice as many turds as a goose does.

The average family drives
each of their cars about 12,000
miles a year, burning about 600
gallons of gasoline and releasing
about 11,000 pounds of See-oh-too
into the atmosphere. This is equal to
about 3,000 pounds of car turds.
The carbon in the See-oh-too released by
driving your family car for a year is nearly twice
the carbon inside the 50-foot-tall maple tree
we met at the beginning of this book.

Learn more about See-oh-too

Are you beginning to see your role in See-oh-too's story?
If we continue to release See-oh-too faster than nature can
turn it into trees, shells, plankton, and more, See-oh-too will
increase his influence on the atmosphere and really heat
things up.

This is already starting to happen. As levels of
See-oh-too increase, glaciers are melting, oceans are
starting to rise, and weather patterns are starting to
change. Animals, plants, and people are beginning to feel
negative effects of too much See-oh-too in the atmosphere.
But you can make a difference, starting today.

Now that you understand how air, trees, coal,
electricity, plankton, gasoline, and humans are all part of
the global-warming story, you can start releasing less
See-oh-too every day.

Here are some simple things you can do to make less See-oh-too:

- Be more aware of when you are releasing See-oh-too. Learn to be aware of him, even though you can't see him, every time you turn on the TV, use the microwave, throw something away, or go for a ride on a motorized scooter.

- Walk, run, and ride your bike. Encourage your parents to drive less.

- Turn lights, televisions, games, and music players off when you are not using them.

- Replace regular lightbulbs with LED ones.

- Recycle everything you can. Make it a game to have the least amount of trash on your block.

- Give extra clothes and toys away to people who need them, rather than throwing them away. Making new things uses energy, which releases CO_2, so it is much better to reuse what we already have.

- Plant trees and plants and help take care of natural areas in your neighborhood.

- Build a fort, play in the dirt, or watch the stars. These games don't release as much See-oh-too as driving to an indoor playspace.

Glossary

Air: The invisible, odorless, and tasteless mixture of gases that surround the Earth. Air is mostly nitrogen (78 percent) and oxygen (21 percent), with small amounts of water vapor (up to 4 percent), as well as argon, carbon dioxide (See-oh-too), helium, methane, hydrogen, nitrous oxide, and ozone.

Atmosphere: The layer of air surrounding the Earth. The atmosphere insulates and protects Earth by keeping just the right amount of warmth in and shielding Earth from too much of the sun's powerful rays.

Atom: Very tiny building blocks that can bond together to build amazing things.

Bond: A connection between atoms, such as two carbons or a carbon and an oxygen. Bonds are what allow atoms to group together to form molecules, such as See-oh-too. Bonds between different atoms contain different amounts of energy. This energy can be released or used up as bonds between atoms are broken and new bonds are formed.

Carbon (C): Carbon is an atom known for its incredible ability to bond with itself and other atoms to form an amazing number of useful things. Carbon is found in coal, oil, natural gas, trees, diamonds, plankton, and you.

Chloroplast: The place in a leaf where light energy is captured and used to begin the process of breaking up See-oh-too and building tree parts.

Coal: A solid black substance made up of dead, squished tree stuff such as carbon, hydrogen, oxygen, nitrogen, and sulphur atoms.

Combustion: The act of burning something, which usually releases energy in the form of light, heat, or both. When coal is burned, See-oh-too gets his oxygen shoes back and a lot of energy is released in the form of heat.

Combustion engine: An engine that operates by using energy generated when gasoline is burned.

Dry Ice: If you cool See-oh-too down to –78.5° C, he will stop gassing around and form a solid. Dry ice does not melt to a liquid like water ice. It goes straight from a solid to a gas as it warms up, which is why it is so good at making witches' brew look spooky on Halloween.

Electricity: Electricity is the current delivered from coal-fired electrical plants via power lines to homes, offices, and stores. When you plug into an outlet, electricity flows through the plug and into the television, toaster, microwave, or computer.

Gas: When something is in a gaseous state, it is floating in the air around us. When See-oh-too is in his normal state, he is a gas.

Gasoline: A flammable liquid made from refined squished, dead, cooked plankton. It is used as fuel in combustion engines such as those found in chain saws, motor scooters, motorboats, and cars.

Global Warming: A process that happens when See-oh-too and other greenhouse gases accumulate in the atmosphere and trap heat. This causes the average temperature of the Earth to increase, which affects plants, animals, the weather, and entire ecosystems.

Greenhouse Gas: A gas that is known to absorb heat radiating from Earth's surface. See-oh-too, ozone, methane, and water vapor are examples of greenhouse gases.

Molecular Weight: The sum of the weight of all the atoms in a molecule. The molecular weight of See-oh-too is 1 carbon (12) + 2 oxygens (16 each) = 44.

Molecule: The union of two or more atoms. See-oh-too is a molecule made up of one carbon and two oxygens. Water is a molecule made of one oxygen and two hydrogens.

Natural Gas: A mixture of gases, but mostly methane, made from dead, squished plankton. Natural gas also forms in swamps, dumps, and coal seams.

Oil: A combustible (burnable) liquid substance made from squished, dead, cooked phytoplankton. When oil is refined, it is turned into gasoline.

Oxygen: A colorless, tasteless gas that makes up about 21 percent of our atmosphere. Animals use oxygen gas to power cells, muscles, and life. Trees make oxygen gas as they pull See-oh-too's shoes off and make more tree parts.

Photosynthesis: The process of using light energy to turn See-oh-too and water into tree parts or phytoplankton.

Plankton: Microscopic floating plants or animals that can be found in fresh or salt water. Dead, squished plankton may become oil or natural gas if it is buried deeply enough and heated to the right temperature.

Refinery: A place where crude oil is refined into gasoline, which makes it ready to use as fuel for cars, mowers, scooters, and more.

Respiration: The way many living creatures obtain energy from tree parts. Respiration uses oxygen and releases See-oh-too.

Solid: If something is firm and has a defined shape, it is solid. Dry ice is See-oh-too in his solid form. Regular ice is water in its solid form.

Stomata: Holes in the bottom of a leaf that allows air into the leaf and water vapor out of the leaf.

Kirk Johnson

is the Sant Director of the National Museum of Natural History at the Smithsonian Institution in Washington, DC. He is a geologist and paleobotanist known for his scientific articles, popular books, museum exhibitions, television documentaries and collaborations with artists. He is the author of *Prehistoric Journey: A History of Life on Earth* and *Cruisin' the Fossil Freeway*.

Mary Ann Bonnell

is the visitor services manager for Jefferson County Open Space, Colorado. For the past 30 years, Mary Ann has used art, science, and enthusiasm to connect people of all ages to the natural world. She has created scientific illustrations, cartoons, scientifically accurate costumes, and soft sculptures for wildlife refuges, botanic gardens, nature centers, museums, and aquaria.